D0946326

VISITING TEACHING
A CALL TO SERVE

VISITING TEACHING
A CALL TO SERVE

JOHANNA FLYNN & ANITA CANFIELD

Deseret Book Company
Salt Lake City, Utah

©1984 Randall Book Company
©1989 Johanna Flynn and Anita Canfield

All rights reserved. No part of this book may be reproduced in any form or by any means without permission in writing from the publisher, Deseret Book Company, P.O. Box 30178, Salt Lake City, Utah 84130.

Deseret Book is a registered trademark of Deseret Book Company.

ISBN 0-87579-288-X

Printed in the United States of America

10   9   8   7   6   5

The Awakening

"I'm only a visiting teacher," she said, and her head hung low.
"I'm really not very important, I guess I'll not even go.
I'm sure that no one will miss me, no one will really care.
I'll see to my work this morning, instead of going there."

So she hurried around all morning, her home was polished and
    swept;
When stopping to rest for a moment, she sat in her chair and
    slept.
And scarce had her eyelids fluttered, before a vision came to her
    sight;
And standing there before her was a personage clothed in white.

She saw in His hands the nailprints, His brow where the thorns
    had lain,
His side where the sword had pierced it; His face with its look of
    pain.
"I gave you some work to do," it seemed she heard Him say.
"You thought it of no importance, so you stayed home today."

"You did not deliver my message; you did not feed my sheep.
You only swept and polished and stayed at home to sleep."
"Oh, Master," she cried, "forgive me, that I should fail to see.
Had I done it unto the least of these, I'd have done it unto thee."

Anona Tomlinson Peterson

Preface

The settings and names in this book are fictional, but the incidents are factual. We have carefully selected many stories and applied them to the characters.

We have not done this to present a picture of perfection, but rather, one of motivation and inspiration. The attitudes, affections, and ideas these characters portray may help us capture the overall view of some of the problems, challenges, and goals of visiting teaching.

We sincerely hope that you will find these messages comforting and challenging.

As we struggle in our personal callings as visiting teachers, we are continually renewed and strengthened by you, our sweet and noble sisters.

The Call

JOURNAL: ELIZABETH   ENTRY: 015012-EON, KOLOB

Sarah and I are still savoring all the beautiful things we've heard in our new classes. It is hard to believe I only have a little over two thousand years left before I go to mortality and gain my body. The thought of earth life both thrills and terrifies me. I am eager to have a body like Father and Mother. I want to be just like them. And I am truly willing to have the experiences we have been studying about in our classes. I know that the pain and joy, sorrow, suffering and trials are all for our good. No experience is wasted. Mother told me herself these things will make us become more like her and Father.

But the thought of the veil being drawn over my memory frightens me. To think that I shall have no recollection of former friends or birth or my home here is often more than I can bear. It is like being "cut off" from them. But Father says that we aren't cut off, we are just living away from home for a while. He said he will always be there for us; all we have to do is have faith and live worthily. He even said that for every 10 percent of work we do, he will do the other 90 percent and give us all the credit. He loves me so much, I just don't want to disappoint him. The veil sounds so foreign, so distant.

JOURNAL: ELIZABETH   ENTRY: 015131-EON, KOLOB

It seems as though it was just yesterday that the Great Council in Heaven was assembled, and yet.

My heart still pounds as I remember Father presenting his plan, and Satan and Jesus coming forth — Satan to alter the plan and Jesus to uphold it. It is still clear in my mind, as if it were just yesterday, the awful war that followed. I remember vividly the burning in my heart as my name was called and I stepped forward to be counted on the Lord's side. My heart still pounds but then aches as I see many who also stepped forward that day but have lost their way after they were born into mortality. It can easily happen to any of us if we aren't careful.

I can see how perfect Father's plan is. He has provided a Savior who will pay for all the sins that have ever been or ever will be committed, mine included. What a swelling in my heart it brings to know this, to know how much they love me and want me back. I feel great comfort — despite the knowledge of the veil — that repentance on Jesus' name will be a miracle and a blessing.

I guess the greatest fact of all is that I can inherit all Father has. It is possible for me to become like Father and Mother. Mother is so beautiful, so magnificent, so incredibly lovely — I want to be just like her.

My dearest sister in all eternity, my sweet friend Sarah, is such an inspiration to me. We truly communicate heart to heart, woman to woman. We think the same thoughts, we have the same fears and hopes and goals. We both plan to come home.

And yet, there are differences in our personalities that make a bonding friendship. She is strong where I am weak, and I am strong where she is weak. We are a perfect blend of friendship and personality.

Today we learned that we are going to earth within a few years of each other.

JOURNAL: ELIZABETH   ENTRY: 015445-EON, KOLOB

Here I was, selfishly excited yesterday, when I learned I was being born into a family of members of the Church. It never dawned on me that Sarah might not be born into a member family. Today as I was bubbling away about it, she looked so distant and forlorn. When I questioned her, she told me that she was going to be born into a nonmember family, and she would be an only child. She said that this knowledge made her all the more committed to absorb everything she could learn here in heaven. She said, "I am going down to mortality *prepared* to find the truth." Then she looked me eye to eye, as only Sarah can, and said, Elizabeth, I'm counting on you to teach me the gospel when we find each other there."

I will do my level best, because Sarah has taught me so much here, and I'm counting on her there, too.

JOURNAL: ELIZABETH   ENTRY: 015498-EON, KOLOB

In class today we heard from both Joseph and the Savior. Together they began to unfold what living the gospel would be like in the last days. I looked around the Great Assembly Hall and saw the multitude of spirits listening intently. None of them seemed to fear the veil being drawn over their memories. It is very comforting to know that all of us have to go through it, not just a few.

The organized Church on earth in my day will be just like the Savior's church in his day. Of course! Why should it be any different? The past few weeks I've been learning about the priesthood, Sunday School, tithing, officers, teachers, Primary, and the special sisterhood called Relief Society. It will be such a unique and sacred sisterhood on the earth that all the sisters are going to spend a whole year learning about just that. Today Joseph introduced it to us.

He is indeed a noble spirit. He counseled us today about what it would be like in our day. In his mortal life he will suffer mental and even physical persecution. The Saints will be mocked, ridiculed, hated, mobbed, raped, beaten, burned, and even murdered. He said that Satan will do everything in his power to discourage and torment and defeat the restoration of the gospel. Those who are going before me to lay the foundation of the last dispensation are indeed noble and courageous. I honor them.

But Brother Joseph grew quiet after a while and looked at those of us who are coming later. He said he was giving us a warning. He said that we would not have to endure physical persecution, but our test would be a much greater one. I was stunned. What could be worse than being beaten, raped, or murdered? He said it is easy to draw close to God—and easy to work hard in the kingdom—when adversity presses against you. During those times people band together in brotherhood, sisterhood, and work together harder. He said a far greater adversity will be peace and apathy. When people are comfortable, they forget why they were born, he said. They forget that they were born to serve each other, just as Father and Mother serve us. He counseled us against the excuses we would be tempted to say. He gave an example: If one of the Lord's living apostles were to come to one of our stake conferences, and that apostle told us that the Prophet wanted us all to leave for Jackson County by 5:00 A.M. the next morning, only four out of ten would even consider it. And in the final analysis, only one out of ten would actually prepare to go. I was shocked! He said it was because we will be *used* to making excuses. We would excuse ourselves right out of the trip. He even shared some of the excuses:

"Well, when I hear it from the prophet himself, then I'll go."

"I can't possibly go this week because my strawberries are coming on. But we sure will go as soon as we put them up."

"I don't think the Lord would want *me* to go. I'm not all that strong in the church; my husband is the strong one in our family, and I couldn't just up and leave my mother."

"I sure would like to go, but we don't have any money until we get paid next week."

"This could be the real thing. But this is the first we have heard about it. It could just be a trial run, like fire drills in school. Well, John just can't take off work for a drill."

Joseph said we would become masters at making excuses. I could hardly believe it! Many didn't believe him. Now I am really afraid of the veil. What if I excuse myself right out of exaltation.

JOURNAL: ELIZABETH   ENTRY: 015513-EON, KOLOB

Joseph held class today for the sisters only. He counseled us that our standard in every facet of life should be a standard of personal excellence. We are choice daughters of God, and we should look, act, and serve accordingly. He said our yard-stick for serving in our stewardships on earth should never be, "What do I have to do?" or "Is this necessary?" But it must always be, "What can I do, how can I help the Savior and his work on earth?"

He asked how many of us will promise everything we will own, including our gifts, to the building up of the kingdom of God. Every hand went up. He wept as he told us that many will be called but few chosen, because many of us will let that promise be forgotten, even grow cold.

After class, Sarah and I talked for hours about our commitment. We know that our choices on earth must be eternal ones. Sarah pointed out that when we hear these truths in mortal life, those who have made firm commitments will recognize the truth. The Savior himself said that his "sheep" would hear his voice and follow him and his teachings.

Sarah and I are determined to keep our commitments. Nothing is as important to us as getting back home. And home would not be home without all our loved ones. I am so grateful to have a friend like Sarah who loves me so much.

JOURNAL: ELIZABETH   ENTRY: 10160113-EON, KOLOB

Today was the last class we had with Joseph Smith. He introduced a program to us that would be part of the Relief Society. It will be called visiting teaching. It will provide every sister in the Church with a friend, a helper, someone to care. Not one sister need ever feel alone. We need not feel that no one understands or cares. We will be called to be visiting teachers to our sisters, to each other. Our time with each other will be what we make it. Our sisters' needs will be our challenges. Some will need physical help, others spiritual or social help. But all will need something from their visiting teachers. He then asked several sisters who have been given specific gifts to share ideas of how this could be done. Sarah was one who stood up. She said one of her gifts was to be a good listener. She felt she could be of service to her sisters in mortal life by listening to the Holy Ghost, listening to the prophet, and listening to those who need to talk. We were shown many ways that we can bless others' lives with our gifts, our *differences.*

He concluded by saying that we should remember the promise we made to build the kingdom, to not fall prey to excuse-making. Serving means *doing.* We shouldn't let our Relief Society president do the work herself because she is tired of hearing all the excuses.

He said, "This charitable society is according to your nature. It is natural for females to have feelings of charity. You are now placed in a situation where you can act according to these sympathies, which God has planted in your bosoms. If you live up to these principles, how great and glorious! If you live up to your *privileges,* the angels cannot be restrained from being your associates!" (Minutes of the Female Relief Society of Nauvoo, p. 142, archives, The Church of Jesus Christ of Latter-day Saints.)

When he finished, all of us were weeping; he took our breath away. Yes, I want angels as my associates.

What if I lose my way, what if I am an excuse-maker? What if my faith weakens? I told Sarah my deepest fears. She grew sober and looked into my eyes as she held my hands and said, "Elizabeth, I won't let go of you, ever. I'll be there, too. I promise I'll help you." I cried and cried and asked her if she realized that the veil meant no recollection of former friends and birth. Did she realize we would not remember each other?

She said, "Elizabeth, we may forget what it was like here and how we got here. And we may not be able to see friends as they were, but you can't tell me I won't feel your spirit when we meet on earth. I will find you and love you. Together, Elizabeth, *together* we will help each other home. I love you with all of my heart."

I believe her. Sarah is making the fear subside. I will make it now; I know it.

JOURNAL: ELIZABETH   ENTRY: 1117630-EON, KOLOB

Sarah and I held hands and listened with our whole hearts as we attended the last class before the Savior goes down to his birth. He said,

> Every tree that bringeth not forth good fruit is hewn down, and cast into the fire. Wherefore by their fruits ye shall know them. Not every one that saith unto me, Lord, Lord, shall enter into the kingdom of heaven; but he that doeth the will of my Father which is in heaven. (Matthew 7:19-21.)

He told us that by our fruits he would know us, that by our good works he would see our hearts. He would not force us, but let us choose according to our agency. But he warned:

> Verily I say, men should be anxiously engaged in a good cause, and do many things of their own free will, and bring to pass much righteousness;
> For the power is in them, wherein they are agents unto themselves. And inasmuch as men do good they shall in nowise lose their reward. (D&C 58:27-28.)

He commanded us to be anxiously engaged in a good cause, to bring to pass our own righteousness. Sarah and I agreed. We began to see that serving is just as much for us as it is for those we serve, maybe even more. How else can we become like Jesus?

Sarah shared this poem with me written by one of her friends.

> "Go give to the needy
> Sweet charity's bread,
> For giving is living,"
> The angel said.
>
> "But must I keep giving
> Again and again?"
> My selfish, thoughtless
> Answer ran.
>
> "Oh, no," said the angel,
> Piercing me through,
> "Just give till the Master
> Stops giving to you."
> (Genevieve L. Barnes, "Charity.")

The Savior explained to us, "And if it so be that you should labor all your days in crying repentance unto this people, and bring, save it be one soul unto me, how great shall be your joy with him in the kingdom of my Father!" (D&C 18:15.)

And he also taught:

> Verily I say unto you, Inasmuch as ye have done it unto one of the least of these my brethren, ye have done it unto me.
>
> Then shall he say also unto them on the left hand, Depart from me, ye cursed, into everlasting fire, prepared for the devil and his angels:
>
> For I was an hungred, and ye gave me no meat: I was thirsty, and ye gave me no drink:
>
> I was a stranger, and ye took me not in: naked, and ye clothed me not: sick, and in prison, and ye visited me not.
>
> Then shall they also answer him, saying, Lord, when saw we thee an hungred, or athirst, or a stranger, or naked, or sick, or in prison, and did not minister unto thee?
>
> Then shall he answer them, saying, Verily I say unto you, Inasmuch as ye did it not to one of the least of these, ye did it not to me.
>
> And these shall go away into everlasting punishment: but the righteous into life eternal. (Matthew 25:40-46.)

Sarah and I spent several hours after the class in silence, just feeling his love for each of us.

JOURNAL: ELIZABETH   ENTRY: 118521-EON, KOLOB

Tomorrow Sarah and I plan to meet by the seventh fountain near the twelfth column in the Great Assembly Hall. We are going early so we can find each other in the multitude. All of us here are anxious to witness the next three days. Father and Mother have told us that the Savior's atonement will mean even more to us who are yet unborn if we are to witness it personally.

Sarah has been such a support to me these last thirty-three years since the Savior's birth on earth. We have learned so much together. I'm not afraid of the veil anymore and neither is she, for we know we'll be there to help each other. I love her so much.

As I have grown in knowledge, I have grown in understanding. I have come to see the veil as a blessing to mortal life. We *must* go through mortality. We *must* have experiences that will teach us what we cannot learn here in heaven (because we have no physical bodies). Once we are mortal, if we could see how wonderful heaven is, the mortal pain and suffering would be even more intense. But the greatest blessing of the veil is that we will have to walk by faith. Faith is the power of God. As we develop faith I am beginning to see that we will become more powerful in subduing our weaknesses. Walking by faith will teach us to stretch beyond our reach. And unless our reach exceeds our grasp, how can we know of our opportunities?

If we could remember our premortal life all through mortality, we might not stretch ourselves. Then the day would come when we would have to face Father and all we could say is, "I'm not sure if I deserve this reward."

I truly did learn more during those three days than I have in all my existence. The poignant scene of the Savior's last supper with his disciples opened new understandings. I saw that it did for Sarah, too, as we wept together.

Can you imagine how our brother felt, knowing of the impending hour, the mockery, the torture, and pain he must surely suffer? Can you imagine how heavy those hours must have been upon him? It was so touching to watch him with his friends gathered there in that upper room – his apostles, men he had lived with and been a constant companion to for all his ministry. These were his choicest, his anointed. Now, except for Judas who betrayed him, they must carry on. It was so hard for our Savior to bid farewell. He loved them so much. It's beautiful the way he tenderly embraced each one and spent a few private moments individually to express his love and appreciation personally, one-on-one.

I could not hold back the tears as I saw him – the Great Jehovah, our Lord, our Master, the Savior of the World – get down upon his knees with no thoughts of his coming ordeal and lovingly wash each apostle's feet. My heart and mind will never forget what he said: "A new commandment I give unto you, That ye love one another; as I have loved you, that ye also love one another. By this shall all men know that ye are my disciples, if ye have love one to another." (John 13:34-35.)

At that moment I knew he wasn't talking to his apostles alone. He was talking to all of us. I realized that the withholding of love is the negation of the Spirit of Christ, the proof that we never knew him, that for us he lived in vain. It means he suggested nothing in all our thoughts, that he inspired nothing in all our lives.

At that moment I covenanted that when it was my turn to experience mortality, I would live my life so his would not have been in vain. I would love others as he loves me. I do know him. I think everyone present made that covenant. There was an overwhelming feeling as the heavens were silent and everyone felt the majesty of our Lord, Jesus Christ.

I ached and grieved as I saw him bleed from every pore at Gethsemane. I had never seen such a thing. At first I didn't understand. I thought the sins weighing upon him were causing all the suffering. Then I recognized that he was also experiencing great sorrow, that which I have seen accompany sin, the remorse felt after the sin has been committed. I saw my Lord suffer that great sorrow multiplied innumerably. Even though I haven't experienced mortality yet, I know my sins were numbered there, too, and I caused some of that pain. Yet I can take hope and not condemn myself, because I realize I am worth the price he paid or he would not have paid it. We are all worth it. I'm beginning to sense how much we should esteem one another, especially those who have lost their way. I never understood until now why he told the story of the joy of finding the one lost sheep while ninety-nine were safe. I know

I am weak in so many areas. I can now clearly see the road home, and it is stained with his blood. I love him for that.

I could hardly watch as they scourged and flogged him. The cruel whip laced with bits of bone and glass tore open his flesh, and I wished they would stop. With every mocking word and gashing blow, my heart would reconfirm my covenant – "I will love you, my Savior, and try so hard to remember who I am."

As they drove the nails into his hands and wrists and feet, I can remember thinking of the blood everywhere, from Gethsemane, to the beatings, and then on the cross. He literally gave most of his own blood for us.

As he hung there, Sarah and I turned to see Father and Mother. They suffered, too. The looks on their faces were similar to the one on Mary's, and yet there was peace about them. They knew. They knew what that moment meant to the world.

I do not know exactly what mortal life will bring to me. I have a good understanding of some of my challenges there, and I know only too well my own personal weaknesses. But I am grateful for this Brother who loves me so much that he was willing to lay down his life and then take it up again for my sake. I am so grateful for his teachings and gospel that will pilot me through mortality.

And I am no less grateful for those dear brothers and sisters here who will teach and inspire me there. I am especially grateful for Sarah, who can reach my heart like no other. I shall not let the veil end our friendship.

I shall strive with all my heart to serve the Lord, as he has served me.

The Service

JOURNAL: SARAH MARKS ENTRY: APRIL 4, 1965

Am I ever burning mad! I don't know about this new ward we live in. Today Jim stayed home from the office until noon because he wasn't feeling well. Here I am, in our new home ten days, boxes everywhere, eight months pregnant with my first baby, a sick husband, and my visiting teachers unexpectedly ring the doorbell at 9:22 A.M. I was so embarrassed, my house was such a mess.

It might not have been so bad, but they brought all four of their own children as well as a neighbor's child one of the women was tending. After all, the woman was *just* going visiting teaching.

The children worked in teams during the *one hour* visit! Two took turns running in and out, leaving the front door open while the air conditioner kept clicking on and off. Two others took turns opening bedroom doors and exposing clutter, unmade beds, and poor Jim. One little girl kept popping the oven door open as she tried to wear out the light button. I waddled up and down stairs, shutting doors and escorting little darlings from room to room. My visiting teachers didn't seem to notice a thing. When they finally left, Jim said, "Looks like you didn't need compassionate service *before* they came, but *after!*"

I don't even remember their names. They never offered to help, seeing my predicament. Oh, well, I'm not going to feel sorry for myself. Besides, once the baby's born I can get more involved in the ward. Maybe I can even find the nerve to tell them to leave their children home.

JOURNAL: SARAH MARKS ENTRY: APRIL 16, 1965

Here I am, almost thirty-four, with my first baby. I've had such terrible allergies that in the labor I alternated screams and sneezes. Our beautiful little Jennie was born at 1:25 A.M. on April 10—she is so beautiful, and I am so thankful for her. She was breech, and my old bones gave very slowly to accommodate her eight pounds, eight ounces. It was such a trauma to my system that something went wrong, and I left the hospital weighing more than when I went in because of water retention. Every morning I wake up with all the water I am holding plus more. My skin is so tight that my ankles are cracking and bleeding. It is so hot that sweat drips off my elbows. I waddle around the house and wonder why my baby won't nurse.

I am an only child, and I have never been around babies. What should I do? Jennie was the first baby I saw without a diaper on. My breasts are so impacted, and Jennie cries constantly. As a matter of fact, so do I.

Unexpectedly, the doorbell rang today at 11:00, waking Jennie up. Guess who? My visiting teachers. They looked at the bloody ankles and my puffy face and said, "Gee, Sarah, you look awful. And it looks like your little girl has colic. Listen, if there is anything we can do for you, just let us know. The message is about prayer. Remember to pray. Well, we can see you're tired so we won't keep you." And they left! They never even came in!

I vow this night that if I am ever called to be a visiting teacher, I will never say, "If we can do anything for you, just let us know."

JOURNAL: SARAH MARKS   ENTRY: APRIL 18, 1965

Thank heavens for sweet old Mrs. Rice in the house next door. Today she hobbled over and called my doctor. Now, after some medication for me and formula for the baby, I'm feeling better already.

The past three years have turned my life into a busy world.

Here I am, a new wife, new member of the Church, and new mother! Now this move to Jim's new job in a town 2,500 miles from parents and friends has caused me additional need for flexibility. I want to be a good wife, mother, and Church member. Those first few months after I was baptized, I felt so overwhelmed. I looked in awe at those Relief Society sisters who could make their clothes, can their food, and repair anything with a glue gun. I'm just not talented like that.

But I learned that dwelling on the things I can't do impedes my personal progress. The Lord gave each of us gifts. I love that verse in the Doctrine and Covenants: "For all have not every gift given unto them; for there are many gifts, and to every man is given a gift by the Spirit of God. To some is given one, and to some is given another, that all may be profited thereby."(D&C 46:11-12)

Each of us have been given at least one gift "that all may be profited thereby." I'm not sure I know what special gift I've been given, but when I discover it, I'll use it to benefit the Lord. I feel that I promised him that once.

JOURNAL: SARAH MARKS ENTRY: MAY 13, 1965

Today I got a phone call from my *new* visiting teachers. The ward shuffled things around, I guess, and I ended up with two new ones. She said she would like to make an appointment to come over (What a relief!) and get acquainted. I hope they don't bring a flock of kiddies; my house and nerves and new baby couldn't handle it.

JOURNAL: SARAH MARKS ENTRY: MAY 15, 1965

I could hardly believe these two angels that came to my door. I have been feeling so separated lately—a new house, new city, new job for Jim, new baby. My whole life seems upside down. I've been blaming it on being thirty-four, but I guess I'm just shy and nervous like everyone else. But within ten minutes these two visiting teachers made me feel welcome to the city, to the ward, and to motherhood.

In five minutes they saw that I am *still* moving in because of the baby and other problems.

Sister Moore said, "Let me take your baby this afternoon and every afternoon this week so you can devote time to the sorting." Sister Lee said, "I'll bring dinner tonight and tomorrow, and with just the two of you, the leftovers will keep you fed for several days." And to top it all off, she asked what we like to eat.

They asked if the home teachers had been by since we moved in. When I said no, they said they'd see to it that we had them come this month. I believe they will.

And that wasn't all — they left with the baby and all the dirty laundry. Tonight they returned, food, baby, and folded laundry! I got more done today than in the past two months.

They came in neat, with clean dresses, looking as if they were going to church. That really made me feel important, and as if I was important to them. Oh, thank you, Heavenly Father, for two living angels!

JOURNAL: SARAH MARKS   ENTRY: MAY 20, 1965

Sister Moore called today to see how things were going. We had a long and warm conversation. She let me know her phone was open all hours, and that she'd be hurt if I didn't turn to her for help first. She is really a friend. And later on in the afternoon Sister Lee stopped by with brownies and a big hug for me. What strength I feel in them.

JOURNAL: SARAH MARKS   ENTRY: JULY 16, 1965

I cannot believe the service I have received over the past few months from Sister Moore and Sister Lee. They have called, dropped by with an unexpected dessert or pitcher of punch. They have sent me notes of encouragement or praise. They have taken time to prepare meaningful messages each month. And not just for me, but to all the sisters on their route. Last Sunday I heard a story about one of the prominent families in our ward, Barry and Barbara Jones. At one time Barry was not a member, and Sister Moore was one of Barbara's visiting teachers. One day, Barbara called Sister Moore to tell her that her grandfather, who had been like a father to her, had just died. She was very upset. She and her mother were discussing the problem of who would keep her little girls during the funeral when the mother said, "Why not call Sister Moore?" (The Relief Society president had held a visiting teaching convention for the ward just the week before and had stressed the need for compassionate service.)

Sister Moore told her not to worry about a thing. She told her that she and her companion would call soon and discuss how best they could serve. She promised that someone would be with her daughters at 1:00 P.M. Monday for the funeral.

Then she quickly whipped up a salad and took it over to the family. She called the Relief Society president and got permission to organize food for the family for the weekend and for the fifty or so relatives and acquaintances expected after the funeral. They did all the organizing. The delicious food came every day, and in abundance.

Barbara's husband, Barry, was already mellowed toward the Church. His home teacher had brought the crew from building the new chapel over, and they had poured some concrete for the new home he was building. He stood and watched in amazement. Two weeks after the funeral, Barry was commenting on how overwhelmingly generous everyone from her church had been during that trying time. Barbara saw her chance and asked if maybe he wouldn't consider letting their home teacher come and teach him the gospel. Well, no, he wasn't interested in hearing their doctrine, but maybe he did owe it to that home teacher to at least hear what he had to say.

Three months later the home teacher baptized him. Listening to this couple bear their testimonies reveals the working force of love in people's lives. Sister Moore was always there for them.

JOURNAL: SARAH MARKS   ENTRY: AUGUST 20, 1965

When Sisters Moore and Lee came today I asked how they came to be such great visiting teachers. Sister Lee said she believed they had been called to sacrifice, to serve the Lord. She said the more we serve and do, the more we love and are loved.

Then she told me the most incredible story:

Sister Lee had been married for fifteen years to an active member of the Church. One day he announced that he was leaving her; he'd met another woman. He was excommunicated and left town shortly afterward with his new wife. Sister Lee was forced to go to work to support their six children. Eventually she had to sell her home and take a second job. He never sent child support payments, and the state could not find him. With every monthly bill, every illness, every crisis, every teenage problem, every challenge, she grew more and more bitter. Year after year she pushed herself into more loneliness and more despair. She said she had never seen such dark and empty hours. (I could hardly believe it was the Sister Lee I knew!) Eight years went by, and she had become a bitter, hostile, self-centered woman. She felt unloved and unhappy.

Then one day, after complaining to her new visiting teacher, this woman simply challenged her to feel better about herself. "How?" asked Sister Lee. The visiting teacher said, "For the next thirty days go find someone to serve—a different person every day for thirty days. It doesn't even matter if you do it anonymously, just *do it.*"

Sister Lee thought the idea was stupid and forgot about it. But after a few weeks, she wasn't feeling much better, so she decided to give it a try.

After seven days she ran out of people to serve. She'd done something for each of her six children and her mother. She realized she didn't know anyone else's needs. She tried to look around and pay attention, but found herself at a total loss. She called her Relief Society president and was able to take a meal here or there, tend children for an afternoon, and pick up an elderly brother for church one Sunday. But she never found thirty people who might need her.

When this visiting teacher came again, she asked Sister Lee to report. Sister Lee told her she really didn't feel much better about herself, but she did admit that it had taken her mind off her own problems. Now what should she do? The visiting teacher said, "Now double it. Find people to serve for sixty days."

Sister Lee thought she was crazy. If she couldn't find thirty people, how could she find sixty? But she agreed. She called the Relief Society president back and gathered more names. Then she began to canvas the neighborhood. She found an elderly widow down the block trying to weed her garden. Sister Lee showed up every Saturday with hoe in hand and helped the old woman get her lawn in shape. She discovered that a neighbor family was out of town, and she began collecting their newspapers for them. Everywhere she went and everywhere she turned, she began looking for ways to serve.

At the end of sixty days, she told her visiting teacher that it really gave her a rest from her own problems. Sister Lee said she suddenly began to realize how secluded she had been, how out of touch she had been with humanity. Now what should she do?

The visiting teacher said, "Now triple it, do it for ninety days."

Sister Lee looked longer and worked harder. Then she hit upon a great idea. She joined Candy Stripers, a volunteer hospital aide group. At the end of ninety days she told her visiting teacher, "I feel so good about this service, I can do it for 120 days!"

Sister Lee told me that at the end of 120 days her life had been changed. She found that she was useful and *needed*. She found that through service she came to love those whom she served. Then, she said, the miracle happened. They loved her in return. She bore testimony to me that she knew we were born to bless each other's lives. Through service we become more like the Savior.

After they left, a sweet feeling of peace entered my heart. The things she said are true.

JOURNAL: SARAH MARKS   ENTRY: SEPTEMBER 27, 1965

I am so excited! Today I was called to be a visiting teacher. I have three active sisters and one inactive. I will record their names so I can report my progress to myself. I have been so moved by the example of my visiting teachers (I should call them friends) that I want to do just as good a job. Their names are Krista Thomas, Becky Miller, Sue Murphy, and Elizabeth Lowe.

I immediately set up appointments with all except Elizabeth. (She goes by Liz.) She is going to be a hard case. She was not at all receptive. In fact, she said, "What happened to my old visiting teachers? I liked them; they never bothered me." Boy, she is really a tough one! But I won't let this get me down.

I have decided to take this calling seriously and prayerfully. I have written a list of my goals.

I thank my Heavenly Father for this opportunity to grow beyond myself. I shall strive to be worthy of this calling and consider it my duty to:

• attend all my Sunday meetings, Relief Society events, and visiting teaching meetings.

• be spiritually worthy and prepared to take the sacrament.

• set an example of tolerance, kindness, service, clean living, and humility.

• seek the guidance and companionship of the Lord in this stewardship.

• strive to develop and exercise my spiritual gifts as a visiting teacher.

• strive to be honorable.

• love my companion and love each sister we visit.

• dress in a manner that shows my respect for the Savior (whose errand I am about) when I make my visits.

• take no children along for these important visits.

• never go alone for an official visit.

• leave my own troubles at home.

• speak no ill, avoid gossip.

• be a true friend and sister to those we visit and leave them uplifted, cheered, and eager to have me return.

• promote faith in Christ and courage in the face of difficulties.

• be positive in any remarks made about others, especially ward and church leaders.

• look for opportunities to serve and strive to be inspired and exercise wisdom in rendering that service.

• prepare, long before I go, to take a special message and something tangible that is significant.

• pray for my partner before and after our visits, thanking Heavenly Father for this privilege and asking for inspiration.

• always give that special message, adapted to the needs of the one.

• remember that I am my sister's keeper; that I am a daughter of God.

JOURNAL: SARAH MARKS ENTRY: OCTOBER 8, 1965

Found out I'm pregnant again. Have to get going on number two because I started so late. We are thrilled!

JOURNAL: SARAH MARKS ENTRY: OCTOBER 10, 1965

I have done my visiting teaching (at least the first visit; I intend to check up on each sister all month) except for Liz. She keeps making excuses not to see me. I'm not pushing it because I don't want to offend her, but I've got to come up with a way to visit her.

JOURNAL: SARAH MARKS ENTRY: NOVEMBER 30, 1965

Oh — I am so sick! I guess morning sickness is my test. My sweet, wonderful visiting teachers have saved me again. All I do is send them thank you notes. Besides taking Jennie for a couple of afternoons this month so I could rest, they have brought food to poor, starving Jim whose dear wife can't even *walk* past the refrigerator, let alone open it. They brought him a birthday cake and even invited us to Thanksgiving dinner.

I feel bad, though, because I haven't lived up to my goal of being a better visiting teacher. I broke down and sobbed to Sister Moore. I told her what a great example she and Sister Lee were and that I wanted to be the same. I feel like a failure; I didn't even call Liz this month. I confided to Sister Moore that I hate the calling, and I really haven't even tried like I should have.

Bless her heart. She put her arm around me and said, "It takes time, dear." First she bore her testimony to me that she knew the Church was true and that visiting teaching was a special program that the Lord, himself, gave us. She said, "Now dear, do you think the Lord said:

" 'Well, I have them sewing their own clothes, making their own jeans, bread, soap, and candles. They spend four hours a month thinking of new ways to use a Clorox bottle or alphabet cereal and learning how to cook on a wood-burning stove. They have quality family nights on both Sunday and Monday, write in their journals daily, spend twenty-six hours a month on genealogy, sixteen on their family organization and eight on their poems and songs for the Eliza R. Snow contest each spring. They write letters to their senators and representatives and to all the elderly they know. They jog every Tuesday, Thursday and Saturday to enlarge their arteries and have aerobics each Monday, Wednesday, and Friday to enlarge their hearts. They produce a quality garden every year and can, preserve, bottle, or dry everything in sight. They do tole painting on their walls. They make their own slipcovers and drapes out of sheets, clip coupons out of the papers for two-and-a-half hours each night and read their scriptures for an hour before falling into bed.

" 'But I do believe that there might somehow be an afternoon or morning that they could manage to have free. So just in case, I'll have something called visiting teaching.' "

At that point I was laughing so hard I felt better all ready. Sister Moore then went on to tell me what she felt the Savior really said about visiting teaching. She asked, "Or do you think that just maybe the Savior said, 'I know these good sisters are so busy doing the other necessary things of life that often they forget to have true fellowship with each other. Some hardly even know other sisters in their wards. Yet the need for personal contact and friendship and love between sisters is great. Too often they forget part of the baptismal covenant that says they promise to bear one another's burdens.

" 'I know that they are busy providing for their families, living and dead. They cannot be all things to all people. But they can provide much happiness and share each other's burdens. I will inspire the Relief Society president to call teams where the companions can teach each other by example and love. I will inspire her to assign routes where I need special help, and as these visiting teachers come to me in prayer, they will draw even closer to me. Through this strengthened bond I will inspire these sisters in ways that they could not experience in other circumstances. Their own paths will be lighted as they light the way for others.

" 'I can remember all things, and I see the sisters of these wards as they were when we were all together in the premortal existence. Some are only waiting for the love and attention and efforts of others to inspire them to find their way back. *It will not be easy.* My own mission was not easy. But my mission made theirs possible. Now these sisters can show each other the way. The sacrifices they make for each other will not enslave them but will exalt them.' "

She looked me eye to eye and asked if I thought the Savior cared about our visiting teaching duties. She had me there.

I have never, until now, seen this program in this manner.

The Lord is counting on us. He needs us to help him. He knows doing it will be to *our* advantage. For every 10 percent of work we do, he'll do 90 percent and give us the credit.

Then Sister Lee said, "Now you know you cannot run faster than you have strength. The Lord doesn't expect us to be all things to all people. He just wants us to do our level best. He wants us to learn to love each other. The Lord wants us to look to him for help."

She also reassured me that as I pray for inspiration, I will receive it. And the more I serve and do, the more I will love and be loved. (She's a living example of that.)

I felt inspired. I have determined to put myself aside and concentrate on my sisters, especially Liz. This very night I began to pray earnestly for help and inspiration to be a better visiting teacher and to especially help Liz.

JOURNAL: SARAH MARKS   ENTRY: DECEMBER 18, 1965

I'm feeling better; the nausea is subsiding. I have sent Liz a note a week for the past three weeks. I called today; she still won't let me in. What can I do? I'm still praying for an answer.

JOURNAL: SARAH MARKS   ENTRY: DECEMBER 20, 1965

Five days till Christmas. I've fasted two meals in Liz's behalf. Tonight I decided to make some brownies and take them over with a Christmas card. I'll do it tomorrow.

JOURNAL: SARAH MARKS   ENTRY: DECEMBER 21, 1965

Ruth and I had to go twice to Liz's to find her home. She opened the door and looked stern. I introduced us and said simply, "Here are some brownies. I hope we can make brownie

points with you so you'll want us to come back each month."
Then my companion gave her a beautiful ornament she had
made. Liz did not invite us in, but she did break into a big
smile and said, "I love brownies! Thank you, and Merry Christmas!"

I hope this means more success next month.

JOURNAL: SARAH MARKS   ENTRY: JANUARY 1, 1966

A new year! As I think of all my challenges and blessings
of last year, I see that we need each other. How could I have
adjusted so quickly to my new life, home, and roles (and being
pregnant again) without Sisters Moore and Lee? I think of them
when I need help. I desire so much to serve the Lord the way
he wants me to. Over and over on Christmas Day I read his
words: "Inasmuch as ye have done it unto one of the least of
these my brethren, ye have done it unto me." (Matthew 25:40.)

It seemed he had said them to me before. Today I have
lingered over his words, "Feed my sheep."

I realize that my visiting teaching calling is how I will do
this right now. Above all, I must lay the groundwork with my
sisters as I go along. We can't wait until a crisis comes and
then think they'll confide in us. I see Sisters Moore and Lee
have done just that. I would automatically call them if I needed
help or advice. We are *called* to establish this type of heartline
with the sisters in our stewardship. I feel so sorry for those
sisters who are cheated out of loving visiting teachers and say
that they are the last people they'd confide in. It usually means
their visiting teachers haven't become their friends.

That's my goal for this year—to become Liz's friend and
get her back to church. Tuesday, when we go to the temple,
I'm putting her name on the prayer roll. I will fast two meals
a month for her (with my companion) until she's back with

us. That's a promise to the Lord to feed that particular little lamb.

JOURNAL: SARAH MARKS   ENTRY: JANUARY 8, 1966

I called Liz for an appointment. The brownies worked! She agreed to see us next week. I know the prayers and fasting have brought us to this point.

JOURNAL: SARAH MARKS   ENTRY: JANUARY 13, 1966

You know, Liz is really a neat girl! Look at my calling her "girl," and she's only two years younger than I am. She married a lot sooner than I did, married an inactive man. She's never really been active either. She hasn't been to church in six years. She has a six-year-old boy, a four-year-old girl, and a one-year-old boy. She really didn't respond well to the lesson at all; in fact, she kept interrupting to check on her children at play. Ruth and I decided not to give the lesson again until we think she'll be more open. We could tell she grew cold and stiffened as we tried to share the message. It's best to just gain her trust and friendship and let her know we care.

JOURNAL: SARAH MARKS   ENTRY: FEBRUARY 28, 1966

I have tried repeatedly to make an appointment with Liz. She just won't let us come back. Ruth took her a loaf of bread and wasn't even invited in. Today when I called her and jokingly said, "Hey, Liz, it's the end of the month. If we don't visit you, we won't get our reward," she did *not* laugh. Boy, did I feel awkward! It was the wrong thing to say. I guess we came on too strong last time. Tonight I sat down and wrote her a note and told her statistics meant nothing to me. She was my sister whether she let me visit or not, and I cared about her. I hope she'll soften her heart. Oh well, back to the prayers — not much fasting now. I'm afraid this pregnancy is getting to me. Six months down and three to go.

JOURNAL: SARAH MARKS   ENTRY: MARCH 8, 1966

Dear Sisters Moore and Lee made their visit early this month so they could celebrate my birthday on March 20 "in style." Big secrets! They are such fun; even though they are grandmothers, they seem like close sisters to me. That has been such a delight to me, having been an only child.

I opened up again about how terrific they were, but I told how discouraging it was not to be received by Liz because I knew I could be the kind of visiting teacher to her that they are to me. Sweet Sister Lee chuckled and said, "Well, honey, you just have to look at this as though it's a creative challenge." Then she reflected on her most challenging assignment as a visiting teacher. She said, "I once was asked to visit a sister who did not even live in the ward. She was married to a young man who had been born and raised in the ward, and when they married they went to work for the circus. They had to leave their permanent records somewhere, so they chose his home ward. I began to write Lynn every month, and even though her routine was hectic, she found time to answer me on occasion. I was excited to have the association with her.

"Then we learned that the couple was expecting their first child, so we began to plan a shower. Most of the sisters in the ward knew the father or at least his parents, but even the ones who didn't wanted to be part of the fun.

"Right after their daughter was born we had an absentee baby shower. Everything was decorated like a circus, with as many stuffed animals as we could borrow. Everyone brought some kind of gift, and after we had admired them all we wrapped the gifts individually and put them into two large packing boxes and mailed them off to Lynn at the circus's winter quarters in Florida. Lynn later said it impressed all her circus colleagues that members of her church would do this.

"Two years later we were living in Midvale, Utah, and the circus came to Salt Lake City. We got a phone call that Sam and Lynn would leave tickets for us at the box office, and we were invited to either come early or stay late, and they would show us around behind the scenes. What a special evening that was for my children! And what a treat for me to get to meet Lynn after all the letters and time that had passed. I felt a real sisterhood with her and a genuine friendship for her husband.

We can never anticipate all the possible opportunities and experiences that a sister may share with us, so we should give each one our all."

I know what Sister Lee was saying: "Sarah, have you given your all?"

In all honesty I now admit that I haven't. I have said that I have, but inside I have really believed that Liz is a hopeless case. "Creative challenge" Sister Lee calls it? All right! Creative I will be! Look out Elizabeth Lowe. You are coming back to church, and you don't even know it!

JOURNAL: SARAH MARKS ENTRY: MARCH 20, 1966

What a surprise and lovely thirty-fifth birthday this has been! At 10:00 A.M. Jim called from the office and warned me to get my hair done; a special surprise was coming at 11:30. At precisely 11:30 the doorbell rang, and there was Sister Lee. She escorted me and the baby to her car for a "surprise ride." We drove to Sister Moore's, and there I was honored and feted with a birthday luncheon. The guests were all of their sisters that they visit. What a great idea! I discovered that they do this for each sister they visit. Since they have been my visiting teachers there haven't been any birthdays; mine was the first in many months. "Creative." Wasn't that what Sister Lee said? These women practice what they preach. But more importantly, they really love those whom they serve.

The luncheon was simple. Each had contributed something—a salad, rolls, drink, and a light dessert. The gift was simply a handmade card from them with a loving greeting. This short hour together really makes their sisters feel special. I can see how it would do wonders for those shy or inactive sisters or those that they have been trying to reach in a personal way. It's a plan that everyone can enjoy, and a sure way for all to get to know each other better and begin to feel like real sisters. Companions can grow closer together, too.

I am learning a lot and being blessed in the process.

JOURNAL: SARAH MARKS   ENTRY: APRIL 3, 1966

Despite two notes, six phone calls, and one attempt to find Liz home, we didn't get in to see her in March. But her "hard case" act isn't discouraging me. Today a neighbor told me that her daughter is in Liz's daughter's class. Liz's little girl said her mother was starting a garden. This afternoon I bought garden gloves, hand hoe, and a pair of maternity jeans. I arranged for a babysitter for Jennie, and tomorrow I visit Liz.

JOURNAL: SARAH MARKS   ENTRY: APRIL 4, 1966

Boy! The look on Liz's face was classic when up her back walk waddled this slightly pregnant pair of jeans with gloved hands and hoe in position! "Hi, Liz. I came to learn how to garden!"

Either out of pity or total bewilderment, she seemed happy to have me there. I have felt it is important to let sisters feel their worth through their own talents and gifts. Being overwhelmed as a new convert by seemingly "perfect" people has made me sensitive to the gap between many sisters, especially the inactive ones. I want Liz to know that she can contribute to my life, too.

For two hours we worked side by side. We got the beans, corn, and squash in. She talked about children, babies, recipes, families, everything but church. But that is okay. As I left for home, hot tired, dirty, and sweaty, Liz grabbed my arm. She didn't say anything for a minute and then just said simply, "Thanks for coming over." I felt a softening for the first time. I am inspired to keep going.

JOURNAL: SARAH MARKS   ENTRY: APRIL 14, 1966

About a week has gone by since gardening. I called my companion and told her that we must keep weekly contact with Liz. Then I called Liz and told her that Jim had brought me two huge green plants from his office. They were remodeling and gave away all the plants. Would she like one? She was thrilled. Jim and I drove over, and he brought it into her living room. It was so big that he had to turn it sideways to get it through the door. She was delighted. She even asked us to share some lemonade. We kept the visit short and sweet.

Don't want to "wear her out" before I even begin, like the first visit.

JOURNAL: SARAH MARKS ENTRY: APRIL 26, 1966

I have been earnestly and sincerely praying for Liz. With only about seven weeks until my baby is born, I don't want to let go of the momentum or inspiration I am beginning to feel in her behalf. After all, if she really is my sister, then as I pray to our Father in Heaven I know that he'll let me know what his "lost" daughter needs. He loves her so much. She's not listening to him right now, so he'll speak to those who will. I wonder how many inactive sisters he is trying to reach through their visiting teachers.

This evening I called her to ask if anything was coming up in the garden yet. She was so responsive. She told me of her success so far and thanked me again for helping. I could feel her warming up to me.

JOURNAL: SARAH MARKS ENTRY: MAY 3, 1966

Today I made an extra large pan of that gooey chocolate dessert Jim loves. It was my excuse for an "unofficial" visit to Liz. I called her and said that the recipe made too much (as if I'd never made it before) and asked if she would like half of it. When I delivered it, she stood on the porch and said, "Sarah, you're too much! At first I thought you'd fade away like all my other visiting teachers. But you keep coming back— and nine months pregnant! Sarah, you make me feel good when I'm around you. You make me feel like I'm important to you. But you've got to stop all this giving! It makes me feel guilty." After I started breathing again, I said that there was something she could give me. She could let Ruth and me visit her "officially" each month. She opened those beautiful eyes and said, "If that's all it takes to keep up your spirits, you've got a deal!" And we both laughed.

I know the Lord will help any sincere and determined person.

JOURNAL: SARAH MARKS ENTRY: MAY 16, 1966

Ruth and I visited Liz today. We didn't give a lesson; we just visited and looked over the garden. Ruth is moving to another ward, so next month I'll have a new companion. But still, she spied a torn jacket laying on a chair and asked about it. Liz explained that she was giving it away because she couldn't sew. Good old Ruth scooped it up and said she'd mend it and have it back in two days. I know that affected Liz, realizing that Ruth was moving. Ruth is going to be a good visiting teacher to the very end.

JOURNAL: SARAH MARKS ENTRY: MAY 23, 1966

I called Liz and told her that I had just been assigned a new companion, Patti Williams, and that we would like to come over for an introduction next week. She said, "I thought this was going to be a once-a-month deal." I answered her quickly, "So this month it will be one and a half." She actually laughed.

JOURNAL: SARAH MARKS ENTRY: MAY 29, 1966

I'm not sure which will be more of a challenge. Patti or Liz! Patti isn't very committed to visiting teaching, and it was a struggle to get her to come with me to see Liz today. She showed up in a dirty pair of jeans and kept hinting how this visit was really interrupting her day.

I never thought about the challenge a companion could give you. Earlier this evening I talked it over with Jim, and he said to look upon it as an opportunity to be a good example. He warned me of finding fault. He said if we look for the faults in others, we'll surely find them. He is right. Well, it still won't be easy after such a good companion like Ruth.

JOURNAL: SARAH MARKS   ENTRY: JUNE 12, 1966

Yesterday, June 11, at 2:06 A.M., my beautiful little girl, Joy, came into this world. There are no words to describe my intense feelings of partnership with God in bringing her into the world. As I look at my new daughter and think about my little Jennie at home, I have an overwhelming recollection of former friends. These are my sisters, my friends, from the premortal life.

I am beginning to see this unique and mysterious sister-hood to which all women belong. It is a special sisterhood, an intense and sacred "bonding" that women have among themselves.

I am beginning to see this bonding as part of an endowment. It is a gift, an endowment to women. The world may not understand it, but it is a great gift. Men may not understand it because they don't have it. Some people don't believe that it exists. But I do, and I believe that it is eternal.

JOURNAL: SARAH MARKS   ENTRY: JUNE 14, 1966

I came home from the hospital today and found that Sister Lee and Sister Moore are indeed the world's greatest visiting teachers. Jim has been fed, and there is enough food in the refrigerator to last a week. And that is not to mention the sandwiches wrapped in foil in the freezer, ready for lunches or snacks anytime.

They assured me that they will take turns showing up every day this week to take Jennie for a few hours so I can rest. I know they will. They are not the type to just say, "If there is anything we can do, let us know." I love them for that.

I'll bet there are a lot of sisters in the Church who can honestly say that no one has ever brought their dinner or shared a treat for any reason short of calamity or death. I remember returning to a sister's house, after learning she was ill, with a sherbet mix to soothe her sore throat, and having her say that no one had ever done that for her. This good sister had been the mission Relief Society president and was known for her own goodness and kindness all over the mission. How sad it was that no one had thought to lighten her load or express love to her in this way.

I think back to last year when Jennie was born. It was hectic—the months before she was born and the weeks just after her birth, with a new job for Jim, living in a new town, going to a new ward, and caring for a new baby. I could have used a lift. I look at all the times this year when my two angels have rung the bell with an appetizing salad, a nice dessert, even just a pitcher of punch for dinner.

Just before we moved from our last area to this one, Jim came home and asked me if I had been nice to someone. I looked at him with a smirk and said, "No, never." He said that he had had the transmission worked on that morning, and when he went to pay the owner for the labor, the man said he would not take any pay. He said, "My wife was very ill last winter and your wife, Sarah, came to the door and left some sherbet for her. That was all she could eat for days."

After thinking for awhile, I recalled that very incident, when Maxine had been ill. Her little girl had told us about her being sick. I just mixed up the sherbet and took it back that afternoon and forgot about it.

Later, when we were moving and the truck and car were all loaded up with the last of our belongings, Maxine's husband came over and caught my husband in the yard. He gave him a pretty glass vase with a nice pink bow filled with pink flowers. There was a card in it. She thanked me for being nice to her and wished me well in our new home. Than she wrote: "You are the most sincere person I have ever known."

Well, I know that I am probably not the most sincere person she has ever known. But what matters is that maybe she feels that I am sincere. How easy it would have been that cold wintry day to just say to the little girl, "You tell your mother that if there is anything we can do for her, she should just let us know."

JOURNAL: SARAH MARKS   ENTRY: JUNE 18, 1966

Today I called my companion and tried to set up a date to visit our sisters. She said she thought we'd be taking the month off because of the baby. I told her absolutely not! She gave a dozen more excuses, and I told her I'd call, make the appointments, and get back to her.

I think this expectation of "time off" for "legitimate" excuses is just a belief that mediocrity is acceptable behavior.

I have heard some presidents stand and say, "We certainly do appreciate all you sisters are doing. We had 67 percent visited last month, and while we didn't see everyone we know you are doing your best."

These presidents ought to help their sisters realize that they are failing themselves, failing the sisters they are neglecting, and failing the Savior who has called them to feed his sheep. We should all be reminded again of the parable of the lost sheep, of the shepherd who left the ninety and nine and went to look for the one. The Lord is not willing that one of his sheep go unattended. The Lord will bless us for whatever sacrifice it takes to reach that one sister.

I have heard leaders stand up at the first of December and say, "Sisters, I know that this month is going to be hectic and really hard for you to get out, with the holidays and all this bad weather we are having. I know you all have other things to do, and I understand that, so just do the best you can." But at the Christmas season, when we remember the mission of the Savior who came to this earth to live and die to provide the Atonement, the perfect example of sacrifice and love, how can we say we don't have time to be about our Father's business because we have last-minute shopping to do?

Those same leaders say in June, "I know that canning season is coming on now, and with the children out of school, and trying to organize family outings and other summer activities, it will be very hard for you sisters to get out. But just do the best you can." In other words, if you sisters don't ever have anything else to do, anywhere else to spend your money than for gas, or nothing else scheduled and a day to spare, maybe you would like to visit one of your sisters.

Maybe the church that does not require everything from us cannot guarantee us anything. Sacrifice is how we prove ourselves. If we only serve when we have nothing else to do, what are we proving? And do we prove nearly so much on a nice spring day as we do when we have driven the forty-two miles in the cold winter snows?

It is rarely just simply a matter of going or not going. This program has so many facets that we probably will never comprehend them all in this life. But there will be another time and place to review it all.

JOURNAL: SARAH MARKS   ENTRY: JUNE 27, 1966

We visited Liz today. She was the hardest to reach all month. We learned she's been gone for three weeks. I have a feeling there are marital problems. She couldn't believe that I just had the baby, and there I was visiting teaching already.

Patti showed up in Levis again. I didn't have to say anything; she brought it up. She asked why I always wore a dress. I told her a story about a sister who continued to serve as a visiting teacher supervisor when she was ill and homebound. Her Relief Society president reported that, with much effort, this sister put on one of her prettiest dresses before doing the telephoning each month, feeling that this act gave her service importance and dignity as she filled her assignment for the Lord.

I asked Patti if it really mattered that this sister always wore one of her prettiest dresses. After all, she was only going to be talking on the phone. Who would see her? This simple act helped her feel special about her work in fulfilling her calling.

This sister put her dress on with much difficulty because of her illness. Perhaps it is a lot of trouble for us, too. But we may be sure that any appropriate and inspired sacrifice, no matter how large or small, will be noted and rewarded accordingly. Such opportunities to sacrifice come in disguise most of the time. I think that we must watch for them and sacrifice each month. It's great to know you can be counted on. You like yourself more when you are dependable and not just known for the quality of your excuses.

I also told her that I believe that what we wear when visiting teaching does make a difference. Why don't the General Authorities show up in different suit combinations occasionally if it really doesn't matter? Why do they wear dark suits and white shirts? Why must the missionaries wear the same dress? We are called to be a peculiar people (that is, particular, special, or different). We are set apart from the world—by choice—in what we eat and drink, where we go, and what we will or will not do. What better way to let the world know that we are special than to dress in a special manner. When we are engaged in our visiting teaching capacities, we are literally about our Father's work. Like missionaries who are about their Father's work, perhaps we should dress accordingly. We are special, particular, and we should bother to be at our best when we are going out about our Father's business.

I also shared with her that it is an accepted fact that our clothing affects our behavior, and behavior, in turn, can affect our actions. If we look like a frump (and feel that way), we will probably not produce as much good as when we look and feel more special. A fur coat and glass slippers are not necessary, but we can all look fresh and attractive, ready to talk about the spiritual message we have prepared.

I truly misjudged Patti. This young sister said simply, "I didn't know that. No one ever explained it to me like that before."

JOURNAL: SARAH MARKS

Surprise! Tonight Liz brought me a bag of tomatoes from her garden and a pair of pink booties for Joy. I struggled to hold back the tears. I didn't want to embarrass her or anything, but I was so thrilled with this gesture of friendship.

I swallowed hard but could not resist hugging her as she was leaving. Neither of us said a word, but I know Liz was reaching out and giving of herself to me. It is a unique and mysterious sisterhood to which we belong. Women have the ability, mind, and heart to literally pour out love to each other. But because of our own fears and inadequacies we sometimes hold back that special endowment, the one thing that will help conquer those fears and inadequacies. It is God's principle that when you build and raise others, you build and raise yourself. Tonight, I felt love grow.

JOURNAL: SARAH MARKS   ENTRY: JULY 13, 1966

Patti and I visited Liz today. Patti wore a clean, fresh dress. She radiated. She let her barriers down and was of a positive mind today instead of negative. And I came determined today to stop judging her and, even if she wore dirty Levis again, to love her. Meeting each other "spiritually" and spiritually being prepared made all the difference in our visit with Liz. Even though she made it clear that she didn't want the message, she was warm and open. As we were leaving, I saw several boxes of peaches in the kitchen. She said she was going to bottle them tomorrow.

JOURNAL: SARAH MARKS   ENTRY: JULY 14, 1966

This is the true gospel in action. Last night I called my visiting teachers to ask if they could take my children today so I could work as a visiting teacher with my inactive sister. They agreed. I never have asked them to babysit before. They've always sensed my needs and just done it. I have never wanted to abuse their kindness and selflessness. Visiting teachers are not to be our on-call babysitters. But this was an emergency, and they agreed.

I showed up at Liz's about 9:00 A.M., and she was already deep in peaches. She readily welcomed me and put me right to work. At noon we enjoyed the lunch she made and then we bottled all afternoon. We talked and laughed and shared our lives. It was great fun, but more than that, she is beginning to trust me. She more than hinted at marital problems. I simply listened. Often a listening ear is all someone needs. Once I asked Sister Moore what she thought a good visiting teacher was, and she said, "A good listener." That's true! We all have the tendency to talk about ourselves. Visiting teaching is one place we should listen. Maybe being a good listener is my gift.

JOURNAL: SARAH MARKS   ENTRY: JULY 21, 1966

I called Liz today and could tell she was crying. I didn't pry. I opened my pantry and did a "Sister Moore." I made a simple dessert and dashed it over. She invited me in and, after making idle chatter, let a tear creep down her cheek. She told me that she and her husband were contemplating divorce. I leaned on Sister Moore's definition of a good visiting teacher and just listened. When I left, about an hour later, Liz seemed relieved. She took my hand and said, "I really needed someone to just listen. Thank you, friend."

I cried all the way home. I am beginning to really love her.

JOURNAL: SARAH MARKS   ENTRY: AUGUST 3, 1966

Liz and I have been talking on the phone nearly every day since she opened up to me about her marriage. Thursday I was able to suggest that she see the bishop for counsel. I even was prompted to suggest a priesthood blessing. I told her I'd call her home teachers and that even Jim would come over. She seemed to be afraid. I don't think she's afraid of the brethren; she's just uncomfortable because she's been inactive. She hasn't really had any contact with the Church since her teenage years. She asked me to explain the priesthood and blessings again. She was embarrassed. I assured her that it was okay not to understand. I assured her that the Lord loved her as much as he loved the prophet. She looked puzzled.

Then I said the dumbest thing! It just popped out of my mouth. I told her that I felt we'd been friends before, and that we were here to help each other. I felt the Spirit as I said it, but it still seemed so dumb somehow. It only made Liz more dubious. She said, "How could I ever help you!"

I could see I was losing ground and ended the conversation. But we've talked every day, and she is thinking about seeing the bishop.

JOURNAL: SARAH MARKS   ENTRY: AUGUST 8, 1966

Patti and I finished our visiting teaching today early — because Jim and I are going on vacation for three weeks. It will be wonderful!

Patti gave a great message. Two weeks ago she called and asked how I prepare my messages. I told her the message we take to our sisters in an important part of the visit. We need to ponder it and prepare ideas to make it special for each sister.

I told her about all the visiting teachers I've had. When I looked forward to the lesson, and they never gave it, somehow I felt cheated. She said she hated it when the visiting teacher just read the message. It was great to feel her sweet spirit, her desire to excel. It made me want to try harder because she was looking to me as an example, as I look to my visiting teachers as examples. It is true, we inspire one another.

Today it was obvious she had prepared. The message was on doing new things to broaden your talents and skills. She took the labels off some applesauce cans and glued yarn in the shape of a large yarn *U* on each of them. Then, at the conclusion of the message, she told the sister that this was a

U can, and that if she would use the idea, it would help her remember that whatever you want to do, "You Can!"

The Spirit radiated as she spoke, and I could tell that she had spent much time in preparation. It was the kind of moment when you hold your breath to absorb as much of the sweetness as you can.

We decided that it would be a great idea to make a special handout each month. She just beamed with self-esteem as she realized that this golden idea had been all hers. We also agreed we should take turns giving the message at every other house every month. Because giving the message will benefit us as much as our sisters, we will grow from preparing and giving it. And it is interesting to see how different it is each time we present the message as the Spirit guides us.

We also agreed that we should not hesitate to bear our testimony to things we have had experience with and know to be true. We don't have to go to the front of the room, clear our throats and be official about it. Just say, "Yes, I know that Heavenly Father does answer our prayers, and I know that the more we pray the easier it gets, and the more we can learn to recognize the answers that come."

Well, even with all this great effort on Patti's part, we still didn't give Liz a lesson. Even with all my "extra mile" effort to befriend her and help her through her storms, she bristled when we drew near to the message.

I am so discouraged at this point! What more does it require? There are others who need me more who would be more receptive. This is really discouraging.

I need this vacation!

JOURNAL: SARAH MARKS   ENTRY: SEPTEMBER 6, 1966

It was great to get away. I feel like a new woman. But I found out that going on vacation in the body doesn't mean we go on vacation with the Spirit. I couldn't get Liz off my mind. I wrote her a postcard each week.

Yesterday was too hectic, trying to unpack, wash clothes, etc. But today I phoned to check on her. She was excited to tell me that she and her husband had been to a marriage counselor. He wouldn't go see the bishop but agreed to a counselor. They've been four times already, and she said things are looking up. At least they've agreed that they love each other enough to save the marriage. She paid me a great compliment and said she owed this to me. I was touched deeply. But when I hung up I thought, "Sarah, if you're so great, why can't you give her the message each month?"

Boy was I a dreamer, thinking I could reactivate her!

JOURNAL: SARAH MARKS   ENTRY: SEPTEMBER 21, 1966

Today at Liz's house during our "official" visit I really turned to the Lord and silently asked his help. Then I mustered all my courage and told Liz that this was the anniversary of our first meeting. It has been one year since I was called to be her visiting teacher. She said she couldn't believe how time flies. Then I said, "Liz, how long do you think it should take to prepare a visiting teaching lesson?" She said that since she'd never done one, she didn't know but guessed it might take a few hours. I looked her eye to eye and said, "Liz, I've been preparing one year to give you a lesson. Do you think that's enough time, or should I give it more effort?"

There was dead silence.

I thought I'd blown it, and I knew Patti was about to faint right on the spot. Then Liz slowly started to talk. She said she knew that she'd been a "hard case." She told us how afraid she was to let go of her feelings because she was afraid of trying to get her life in order. She was afraid to hear spiritual things because she might realize how far off course she was. And then she admitted that if she realized that, she'd be overwhelmed at the prospect of ever getting back on course.

I looked over at Patti, she was fighting tears. So was I. I told Liz that that's what visiting teachers were all about. The Church is for all of us sinners hoping to become Saints. We are here to help one another become more Christlike. We talked a long time.

She then said, "Okay, if I let you give me the lessons, you aren't going to try to reform me overnight, are you?"

We all laughed. Whew! It broke the ice. I told her that it was *never* our intention to reform her. We love her like she is. Then Patti told her that we have found that the gospel messages make us happier and that sharing them helps make others happier, too.

She accepted that.

Tonight I feel like I have just started climbing Mt. Everest.

The Blessing

JOURNAL: ELIZABETH LOWE   ENTRY: MARCH 2, 1984

There is so much in my heart tonight that I cannot keep the tears from flowing freely.

My visiting teachers, Anne and Vicki, just left after helping me with the dishes. They told me that it was the most beautiful missionary farewell they had ever been to. I know that John is my son, but that's how I felt, too. Almost every member of our ward came to the open house tonight, and the comments were unbelievable.

"The Spirit was so strong."

"John bore a powerful testimony."

"You and Brother Lowe are great examples to all of us."

"Your son truly is representative of a son of God."

"This was the first sacrament meeting my teenage son listened to in six months."

And those are only a few of the comments. I know they meant it; many eyes were glistening. The spirit was so strong!

Tomorrow we leave to drive John to the MTC in Provo, Utah. I will miss my handsome son, my last baby. But I know that he has been called to Spain by the Lord to do his work. John's enthusiasm for life and the gospel will make him a great missionary. Spain will never be the same again!

It seems like only yesterday that Eric left on his mission, my firstborn and first to leave home. I shall treasure the letters from those wonderful people in England that he baptized. When the first letter came, I realized how mighty one testimony truly is. I realized for the first time how powerful the force of love is.

The testimony and love of Sarah. Oh, Sarah, how I wish you were here to see all this and realize the great influence you have been in this world. But I can only hope that across the veil you have been permitted to see the force for good that you were in this life. Tonight's compliments belonged to my dear and beloved friend, Sarah.

It was Sarah who was not afraid to reach out to a rebellious and bewildered sister who was afraid to search her own soul. It was Sarah who knew how to simply listen to another's anguish and then reassure with love and confidence. It was Sarah who was not afraid to bear her testimony of the living God who can work miracles—and is eager to. It was Sarah who loved me back into the gospel, back into the arms of the Savior. It was Sarah who helped me see that once in his arms, he would love me back into the presence of my Heavenly Parents. I love her for that. I miss my old friend.

I'll never forget the Saturday in September she called and said, "Well, it took me one year before I could give you the visiting teaching lessons, now it's taken me another year to get you to come to church. I'll be by to pick you up at 9:15 on Sunday." She then hung up, and I knew I was coming back. I knew Sarah wouldn't let me go. I knew she thought I was worth saving.

I shall also never forget those struggles of that first year of activity. Small things got me down. I felt so unworthy of all the others sisters. Frank wouldn't have anything to do with the Church, either. And sometimes I felt like hiding rather than going to church alone with the kids. Sarah sensed my needs. I remember how embarrassed I was when she mentioned in one of her visits that she was making cookie trains for Christmas and would be happy to show me how. I didn't want to hurt her feelings, but I wasn't about to be pushed into another corner of failure. I had sat on the dunce stool too many times already from too many of those cute little homemaking projects that they swore "anyone can do because they are so simple." And my files bulged with copies of everyone's bread recipes that would never fail. I sure proved them wrong.

But Sarah persisted. I tried hard but never could get annoyed with her because she was so nice. She would call every other day and say, "What are doing today? Wouldn't you like me to come over and make you a cookie train?" or "Why don't you get the supplies and let me show you how to make the first one! I have two whole hours today reserved just for you." Well, she really did have me over a barrel, because I knew her schedule was very busy. Yet with everything that she was involved in, Sarah was constantly willing to set aside time to help me. Didn't her sweet attitude obligate me?

One day I did finally agree to let her make me a cookie train while I watched. She was a great teacher, full of patience, careful to tell me little hints as she went along, and she was careful not to force me to try it. She may have been a little discouraged when she left because I had been adamant in saying that I, who might as well have feet where my hands should be, would never be able to hold an icing bag and get it to do all the cute little things that she did.

Ah, but after Sarah left, I looked at all those leftover cookies and the pot of royal icing, and I could not resist just trying one lousy little cookie train. I worked feverishly into the night, stopping only to race to the all-night grocery and buy more and more cookies. And eventually, guess what? I made thirteen cookie trains to give away that Christmas!

Not only did that rekindle some confidence in myself and lift my spirits, but I actually became an expert at something for the rest of my life.

I'm so glad Sarah stuck with me. We used to laugh about her early visits — all the times I left the TV on while she tried to talk, the appointments I never kept, taking the phone off the hook the day she was to call, and on and on.

Frank was so hostile to her in those months of my reactivation. I guess he thought he was "losing" me. After all, we had just patched up a very bruised marriage. He was downright rude to her. I remember when I was sick once and she came to the door with dinner. She told me later that she had stood on the front porch and prayed five full minutes before ringing the bell. Then Frank opened the door and roared, "What is this? You don't have to bring us charity. We're not a welfare case!"

She came right back at him: "Oh, Brother Lowe, you know I know that it isn't necessary. I'm just here because I love Liz, and I thought this might be one way I could show it. Even if you just take it in and put it straight into the garbage, I had to bring it. I know how I feel when I'm sick. I'm just showing my love for your family."

And, of course, it was Sarah who was there when we lost our precious little Lisa. It seemed like only moments after the accident that Sarah was there, but I know several hours must have passed. She was there with words of love and comfort. I felt all the strength go out of her and come into me. Both she and Jim never left Frank and me wondering where to turn next. They took the boys while we went to the funeral home. They ran all the errands in preparation for the funeral. She even got Frank's suit pressed and arranged for all the food.

Somehow, in those dark hours we knew that Jim and Sarah were there for us, as near as the phone, and that we could count on them.

A few weeks after the funeral, Bill and Sarah came over with a beautiful painting of Lisa, dressed in white running toward us. Most people would have been afraid to give such a gift, but not these inspired people. They had had a friend paint it from Lisa's school picture.

As they presented it to us, Sarah said, "It's called 'Resurrection Morning,' and we are here to tell you how this scene can really happen." It was the turning point in Frank's life. He listened with a sincere and softened heart. The Spirit was there in full force. We felt it bear witness that what was said was true. That night, for the first time ever, Frank and I knelt in prayer together. With hands clasped, we promised the Lord we would be a "forever family." One year later it was Sarah who knelt as proxy for Lisa as we were sealed for all eternity in the temple of the Lord.

The night Sarah died, Frank held me and told me that he felt sure that our little Lisa had met her on the other side and personally thanked Sarah for all she had done for our family. I wept all that night, not for sorrow, even though I would miss her, but because Sarah had helped make it possible that we would be with our little Lisa again.

Who will ever forget the impact she had on our ward when she was called to be the Relief Society president? When we had our first women's conference in September 1978, one of the speakers made the statement that President Kimball wasn't just *our* prophet, but was the prophet of all women on this earh. This statement went right to her heart. She couldn't forget the idea that she was the Relief Society president for all the ladies living within her ward boundaries. She discussed this with the bishop, counselors, and the sisters of her ward, and they all agreed to canvas the ward boundaries and ask all non-LDS women living there if they would like to have visiting teachers. They explained exactly what the function of a visiting teacher was and suggested that if it were agreeable, a pair would call on them once a month. All but two women expressed interest in having such a visit. Sarah said she felt those two had the right to refuse the invitation and that the angels would so record it so that she would no longer be held accountable for not tending to their needs.

But she was excited to see that every other sister was agreeable, and each visiting teaching team in her ward now had the opportunity to truly lengthen their own strides as they took on more sisters and expanded their routes to much heavier loads. As with anything in the gospel, the harder they worked, the greater were the blessings they earned.

The nonmembers began to turn to their visiting teaching sisters, just as is supposed to happen when the program is working. There were many examples of their success. One

woman called and said that her mother was ready to fly back
East after being with her and her new baby for a time. They
had appreciated the meal that had been brought in by the
visiting teachers, and the mother had enjoyed visiting with the
sisters, too. Now the reservation for her flight was made, but it
was at an hour when the husband could not take her to the
airport. Could their visiting teachers help out? What a marvelous victory for these two sisters, to know that they had been
faithful enough that this lady felt free to turn to them when
she needed them.

And what a marvelous tribute to Sarah. She lived what she
used to teach us:

> Not what we give, but what we share,
> For the gift without the giver is bare.
> Who gives of himself with alms feeds three:
> Himself, his hungering neighbor, and me.
> (James Russell Lowe,
> "Vision of Sir Launfall.")

During the short two years she was president, no sister
who was ill went without care, no new mothers went without
meals, no one moved in or out of the ward without help. She
didn't chastise us, she loved us into serving. She encouraged
us to do everything with love and excellence. She inspired us
with ideas to be great visiting teachers, simple Christlike ideas
such as tending children, sending notes, paying attention to
other's accomplishments, being tactful, bearing testimonies,
remembering birthdays and holidays, being positive, always
visiting, preparing good lessons, being there in sickness or
disaster, and bringing food — always bringing food! And not
just food but beautiful food. After all, Sarah believed that every
act of service was for the Lord. She wondered if sisters thought
that what food looks like didn't matter. She told us to watch
at the next potluck dinner and see which bowls empty the
fastest.

She would say, "They will always be the ones where the parsley is outlining the potato salad, and there is a big daisy in the middle made out of long slices of a hard-boiled egg. At Christmas, the platter of date-nut bread won't go first unless it is decorated with artificial holly. Instead, it will be the iced cookies or iced gingerbread men. People will take those iced gingerbread men even when they don't like gingerbread, just because of the eye appeal. At summer picnics the first bowl emptied won't be the beans baked in one of those old glass bowls that looks like it crossed the plains in 1847 and has been used over open fires."

Sarah always taught us to never say, "If you need anything, please call," but to ask ourselves, "What would the Savior have me do here?" Sarah taught that "charity never faileth."

Sarah was an ordinary woman who struggled to overcome her weaknesses and inadequacies like each of us. But she truly believed that the Lord had called her to serve her brothers and sisters. She always quoted: "And behold, I tell you these things that ye may learn wisdom; that ye may learn that when ye are in the service of your fellow beings ye are only in the service of your God." (Mosiah 2:17.)

Well, I have rambled on, and it is late into the night, but I want my sons and their children and all my posterity to know that this great woman influenced my life, so that instead of becoming a mother of generations of apostates, I am now becoming a mother of generations of faithful Latter-day Saints. I want my posterity to know that this special day—John's missionary farewell—was possible because of a devoted, dedicated and loving visiting teacher.

I want my posterity to know that Eric's mission and his temple marriage were also possible because of this woman's testimony in my life. There are members in England (and soon Spain) whose children and their children and on and on will come to the Lord Jesus Christ because of Sarah. And the ripple effect goes even beyond the veil. Frank and I are doing our genealogy and seeing work done for our kindred dead. So it is true—one person does make a difference.

Often I have longed for her friendship and counsel. Ours was a perfect blending of friendship and personality. She was strong where I was weak, and maybe I was strong where she wasn't. Now that I am Relief Society president, I feel the burden heavy on my back for all the "sheep" of this, His fold.

Sarah, thank you for teaching me that perhaps no calling requires better judgment, keener insight, more prayerful preparation, deeper sincerity or more love than that of a visiting teacher.

I wish she could have been here today to share these moments with us. If she had been, I know she'd be busy making sure our needs were met. I believe that she is sharing it in another way. Wherever Sarah is, I know she's serving still. She is truly becoming like the Master.

She's been gone five years now, and I miss her so much. But when she died, when the illness that she had never spoken of, had never burdened others with, finally overcame her, she sent a message to me. Jim told me that she said, "Tell Liz I'll put in a request to live on the same block with her in the celestial kingdom."

I look forward to that reunion. She believed I could make it!

I tremble to think what might have happened if she'd given up on me.

I have only one regret—I never told Sarah something that always seemed so right. I feel like I have known her always . . .

Points to Ponder

True or False   1. Being a visiting teacher is an opportunity for me to grow and sacrifice, and I welcome the challenge.

True or False   2. Visiting teaching should be assigned to sisters who don't have anything else to do.

True or False   3. I would never be ashamed for the Savior to see how I look when I am on my way visiting teaching.

True or False   4. If I have been to a sister's home and she is not there or won't let us in, I feel like I have done my part; I did make an honest effort.

True or False   5. I have prayed for those in my district, apart from those prayers offered with my partner before we go out.

True or False   6. I have fasted for those I visit.

True or False   7. I do not think it is absolutely necessary to always give the official message.

True or False   8. If the sister we visit has already been out visiting teaching herself that month, we usually do not give the message.

True or False   9. I have never volunteered to take the children of one of my sisters.

True or False   10. I have never taken dinner to any of my sisters unless it was assigned by the Relief Society president.

True or False   11. My partner and I do not make a practice of taking something to each sister every single time we do our visiting teaching.

True or False   12. I don't think it matters, so if my partner and I cannot make connections, it is perfectly fine to go alone.

True or False   13. I do not see that attending my other meetings on Sunday has any connection with my being a visiting teacher.

True or False   14. I have never left a note for a sister just to say we had been there to visit and were sorry to have missed her.

True or False   15. I have no other contact with my sisters except when I visit them. My companion and I have never had lunch with them or done anything socially.

True or False   16. I have never borne my testimony to the sisters I visit.

True or False   17. I go into each home every month looking for a chance to serve.

True or False   18. I do not have the money to be the kind of visiting teacher I would like to be. I just can't afford the casseroles, etc.

True or False   19. I have never written any of my sisters or any member of her family.

True or False   20. I honestly don't think visiting teaching is necessary. I think some other program could be more effective and could make use of our time more wisely.

True or False   21. If the sister and I have nothing in common and she is inactive, I don't think I should have to bother her every month. It is a waste of time for us both and is also embarrassing.

True or False   22. Most of the time I think the Relief Society president isn't fair, or just isn't thinking, when she assigns the districts and decides who will be companions.

True or False   23. I don't believe that my little visits every month will really change anybody's life.

True or False   24. I do believe that our visits are spiritual, our example is good, we are sincere, and we are consistent—so it is possible that these sisters will want to improve themselves, too.

True or False   25. I am willing to be judged today on the quality of my visiting teaching.

True or False   26. I am really committed to the visiting teaching program.

True or False   27. I really believe that the visiting teaching program is inspired.